HANGOVER

Helper

Publications International, Ltd.

Pictured on the front cover: Waffled Breakfast Hash *(page 28).*

Pictured on the back cover *(clockwise from top left):* Pulled Pork Sandwiches *(page 76),* Grilled Chicken Tostadas *(page 116),* Quick Jelly-Filled Biscuit Doughnuts *(page 20)* and Spaghetti & Meatballs *(page 136).*

ISBN: 978-1-68022-981-3

Library of Congress Control Number: 2017937553

Manufactured in China.

8 7 6 5 4 3 2 1

Microwave Cooking: Microwave ovens vary in wattage. Use the cooking times as guidelines and check for doneness before adding more time.

Preparation/Cooking Times: Preparation times are based on the approximate amount of time required to assemble the recipe before cooking, baking, chilling or serving. These times include preparation steps such as measuring, chopping and mixing. The fact that some preparations and cooking can be done simultaneously is taken into account. Preparation of optional ingredients and serving suggestions is not included.

Table of Contents

Cinnamini Monkey Bread

MAKES ABOUT 16 SERVINGS

3 cups all-purpose flour, plus additional for work surface

1 package (¼ ounce) rapid-rise active dry yeast

1 teaspoon salt

1 cup warm water (120°F)

2 tablespoons butter, melted

5 tablespoons butter, very soft, divided

½ cup packed brown sugar

2 teaspoons ground cinnamon

¼ teaspoon coarse salt

1 cup powdered sugar

2 ounces cream cheese, softened

3 tablespoons milk

1. Combine 3 cups flour, yeast and 1 teaspoon salt in large bowl of stand mixer. Stir in water and 2 tablespoons melted butter to form rough dough. Knead with dough hook at low speed 5 to 7 minutes or until dough is smooth and elastic.

2. Shape dough into a ball. Place in greased bowl; turn to grease top. Cover and let rise in warm place about 1 hour or until doubled in size.

3. Grease 12-cup (10-inch) bundt pan with 1 tablespoon soft butter. Combine brown sugar, cinnamon and coarse salt in shallow bowl. Turn out dough onto lightly floured surface. Roll dough into 24×16-inch rectangle; cut lengthwise into four strips.

4. Spread 1 tablespoon soft butter over each dough strip; sprinkle evenly with cinnamon-sugar, pressing gently to adhere. Starting with long side, roll up dough jelly-roll style; pinch seam to seal. Cut crosswise into 1-inch slices; place slices in prepared pan with cut sides of slices against side of pan. Cover and let rise in warm place 30 minutes or until dough is puffy. Preheat oven to 350°F.

5. Bake 20 to 25 minutes or until bread is firm and lightly browned. Loosen edges of bread with knife; immediately invert onto large serving plate. Cool slightly.

6. Meanwhile, for glaze, whisk powdered sugar, cream cheese and milk in medium bowl until smooth. Drizzle over bread. Serve warm.

Tip: Serve remaining glaze with bread for dipping.

Chorizo-Potato Hash with Crisp Crumb Topping

MAKES 6 SERVINGS

1 naan bread, torn into uneven pieces

6 tablespoons plus 1 teaspoon olive oil, divided

Kosher salt and black pepper

1 pound Mexican chorizo, casings removed

1 onion, diced

1 yellow bell pepper, diced

1 red bell pepper, diced

2 russet potatoes, peeled, shredded, rinsed and squeezed dry *or* 1 bag (1 pound 4 ounces) refrigerated shredded hash brown potatoes

1 green onion, sliced on the bias

1. Place naan pieces in food processor or blender; pulse until small crumbs form, about 15 pulses. Remove to large bowl; toss with 2 tablespoons oil.

2. Heat large skillet over medium heat. Add crumbs; cook 6 to 8 minutes or until browned and toasted, stirring occasionally. Season with salt and black pepper; set aside.

3. Heat 1 teaspoon oil in same skillet over medium-high heat. Add chorizo; cook about 5 minutes or until browned, using spatula to break up meat. Remove to paper towel-lined plate. Heat 1 tablespoon oil in same skillet. Add onion and bell peppers; cook 8 minutes or until tender, stirring occasionally. Season with salt and black pepper. Remove to bowl.

4. Heat remaining 3 tablespoons oil in same skillet. Add potatoes in even layer; cook 3 minutes or until browned and beginning to crisp on bottom. Turn potatoes; cook about 10 minutes or until tender and evenly browned, stirring occasionally. Season with salt and black pepper. Stir in chorizo and onion-bell pepper mixture; cook 2 minutes or until heated through. Top with naan crumbs and green onion to serve.

Tip: This recipe is especially good to make when you have day-old or stale flatbread.

Oatmeal with Maple Glazed Apples and Cranberries

MAKES 4 SERVINGS

3 cups water

2 cups quick or old-fashioned oats

¼ teaspoon salt

1 teaspoon unsalted butter

¼ teaspoon ground cinnamon

2 medium red or golden delicious apples, unpeeled and cut into ½-inch pieces

2 tablespoons maple syrup

4 tablespoons dried cranberries

Slow Cooker Directions

1. Combine water, oats and salt in slow cooker. Cover; cook on LOW 8 hours.

2. Meanwhile melt butter in 10-inch nonstick skillet over medium heat. Stir cinnamon into butter. Add apples; cook and stir 4 to 5 minutes or until tender. Stir in syrup; heat through.

3. Spoon oatmeal into four shallow bowls; top with apple mixture and dried cranberries.

Caramelized Bacon

MAKES 6 SERVINGS

12 slices (about 12 ounces) applewood-smoked bacon

½ cup packed brown sugar

2 tablespoons water

¼ to ½ teaspoon ground red pepper

1. Preheat oven to 375°F. Line 15×10-inch jelly-roll pan with heavy-duty foil. Spray wire rack with nonstick cooking spray; place in prepared pan.

2. Cut bacon in half crosswise, if desired; arrange in single layer on prepared wire rack. Combine brown sugar, water and ground red pepper in small bowl; mix well. Brush generously over bacon.

3. Bake 20 to 25 minutes or until bacon is well browned. Immediately remove to serving platter; cool completely.

Note: Bacon can be prepared up to 3 days ahead and stored in the refrigerator between sheets of waxed paper in a large resealable food storage bag. Let stand at room temperature at least 30 minutes before serving.

Devil's Food Pancakes

MAKES ABOUT 22 (4-INCH) PANCAKES

Strawberry Topping
(recipe follows)

1 package (about
15 ounces) devil's
food cake mix

2 cups milk

2 eggs

½ cup mini semisweet
chocolate chips

Powdered sugar

1. Prepare Strawberry Topping.

2. Whisk cake mix, milk and eggs in large bowl until well blended. Stir in chocolate chips.

3. Heat griddle or large nonstick skillet over medium-low to medium heat.* Pour ¼ cupfuls batter onto griddle. Cook 3 to 4 minutes or until edges appear dry; turn and cook 2 to 3 minutes.

4. Sprinkle with powdered sugar and serve with Strawberry Topping, if desired.

If using electric griddle, do not cook pancakes at higher than 350°F as they burn easily.

Strawberry Topping: Combine 1 cup chopped fresh strawberries and ⅓ cup strawberry preserves in medium bowl; stir to blend.

Note: These pancakes freeze well. Freeze four pancakes in large resealable food storage bag. Reheat in the microwave oven as needed.

Ham & Egg Breakfast Panini

MAKES 2 SANDWICHES

Nonstick cooking spray

¼ cup chopped green or red bell pepper

2 tablespoons sliced green onion

1 slice (1 ounce) smoked deli ham, chopped

2 eggs

Black pepper

4 slices multigrain or whole grain bread

2 slices (¾-ounce each) Cheddar or Swiss cheese

1. Spray small skillet with cooking spray; heat over medium heat. Add bell pepper and green onion; cook and stir 4 minutes or until crisp-tender. Stir in ham.

2. Whisk eggs and black pepper in small bowl until well blended. Pour egg mixture into skillet; cook 2 minutes or until egg mixture is almost set, stirring occasionally.

3. Heat grill pan or medium skillet over medium heat. Spray one side of each bread slice with cooking spray; turn bread over. Top 2 bread slices with 1 cheese slice and half of egg mixture. Top with remaining bread slices.

4. Grill 2 minutes per side, pressing down lightly with spatula until toasted. (Cover pan with lid during last 2 minutes of cooking to melt cheese, if desired.) Serve immediately.

Hawaiian Bread French Toast

MAKES 8 TO 10 SERVINGS

6 eggs

1 cup milk

1 cup whipping cream

2 teaspoons coconut extract

2 teaspoons vanilla

1 teaspoon ground cinnamon

¼ cup sugar

1 pound sliced sweet Hawaiian rolls or bread, sliced lengthwise and cut to fit slow cooker

2 tablespoons unsalted butter, cubed

½ cup flaked coconut, toasted*

To toast coconut, spread in single layer in heavy-bottomed skillet. Cook and stir over medium heat 1 to 2 minutes until lightly browned. Remove from skillet immediately. Cool before using.

Slow Cooker Directions

1. Coat inside of slow cooker with nonstick cooking spray. Whisk eggs, milk, cream, coconut extract, vanilla, cinnamon and sugar in large bowl.

2. Place bread in slow cooker; dot with butter. Pour egg mixture on top; press bread down to absorb egg mixture. Cover; cook on HIGH 2 hours. Sprinkle with toasted coconut.

Corned Beef Hash

MAKES 4 SERVINGS

2 large russet potatoes, peeled and cut into ½-inch cubes

½ teaspoon salt

¼ teaspoon black pepper

¼ cup (½ stick) butter

1 cup chopped onion

½ pound corned beef, finely chopped

1 tablespoon horseradish

4 eggs

1. Place potatoes in large skillet; add water to cover. Bring to a boil over high heat. Reduce heat to low; simmer 6 minutes. (Potatoes will be firm.) Remove potatoes from skillet; drain well. Sprinkle with salt and pepper.

2. Melt butter in same skillet over medium heat. Add onion; cook and stir 5 minutes. Add corned beef, horseradish and potatoes; mix well. Press mixture with spatula to flatten.

3. Reduce heat to low; cook 10 to 15 minutes. Turn hash in large pieces; pat down and cook 10 to 15 minutes or until bottom is well browned.

4. Meanwhile, bring 1 inch of water to a simmer in small saucepan. Break 1 egg into shallow dish; carefully slide into water. Cook 5 minutes or until white is opaque. Remove with slotted spoon to plate; keep warm. Repeat with remaining eggs.

5. Top each serving of hash with 1 egg. Serve immediately.

Quick Jelly-Filled Biscuit Doughnuts

MAKES 10 DOUGHNUTS

1 can (about 7 ounces) refrigerated biscuit dough (10 biscuits)

⅓ cup coarse sugar

1 cup strawberry preserves*

*If preserves are very chunky, process in food processor 10 seconds or press through fine-mesh sieve.

1. Pour about 2 inches of oil into Dutch oven or large heavy saucepan; clip deep-fry or candy thermometer to side of pot. Heat over medium-high heat to 360° to 370°F.

2. Separate biscuits. Place sugar in medium bowl. Fry dough in batches 1 minute per side until puffed and golden. Remove to prepared wire rack. Immediately toss in sugar to coat.

3. Fit piping bag with medium star tip; fill bag with preserves. Poke hole in side of each doughnut with paring knife; fill with preserves. Serve immediately.

Scrambled Egg Pile-Ups

MAKES 1 SERVING

2 eggs

2 tablespoons milk

Salt and black pepper

¼ cup diced orange bell pepper

1 whole green onion, thinly sliced

¼ cup grape tomatoes, quartered (about 6 tomatoes)

⅓ cup (about 1½ ounces) shredded Cheddar cheese

1 to 2 tablespoons sour cream (optional)

1. Preheat waffle maker to medium; coat with nonstick cooking spray.

2. Whisk eggs and milk in small bowl. Season lightly with salt and black pepper. Working quickly, pour egg mixture onto waffle maker, sprinkle with bell pepper, green onion and tomatoes. Close; cook 2 minutes or until puffed.

3. Remove "waffle" to plate; sprinkle with cheese and top with sour cream, if desired. Serve immediately.

Tip: To remove from waffle maker, place a plate over the egg and flip the egg onto the plate. Or, use the tip of a fork to gently release egg from waffle maker, then slide a wide spatula under to gently remove.

Serving Suggestion: For a hearty breakfast, serve with hash brown potatoes and bacon.

Banana Walnut Muffins

MAKES 12 MUFFINS

½ cup (1 stick) unsalted butter, softened

1 cup packed light brown sugar

2 eggs, at room temperature

1 teaspoon vanilla

3 ripe bananas

¼ cup sour cream

2 cups all-purpose flour

2 teaspoons baking powder

½ teaspoon baking soda

½ teaspoon ground cinnamon

¼ teaspoon salt

¼ teaspoon ground nutmeg

1 cup coarsely chopped walnuts, toasted*

To toast walnuts, spread in single layer on baking sheet. Bake in preheated 350°F oven 8 to 10 minutes or until golden brown, stirring frequently.

1. Preheat oven to 375°F. Line 12 standard (2½-inch) muffin cups with paper baking cups or spray with nonstick cooking spray.

2. Beat butter in large bowl with electric mixer at medium speed until soft and fluffy. Add brown sugar; beat until blended. Whisk eggs and vanilla in small bowl. Gradually add to butter mixture, blending well after each addition.

3. Mash bananas in medium bowl. Add sour cream; beat until smooth. Add banana mixture to egg mixture; beat until smooth.

4. Whisk flour, baking powder, baking soda, cinnamon, salt and nutmeg in large bowl. Gradually add to egg mixture, stirring just until blended after each addition. Stir in walnuts. Spoon batter evenly into prepared muffin cups.

5. Bake 25 minutes or until toothpick inserted into centers come out clean. Cool on wire rack. Store in airtight container between sheets of waxed paper at room temperature up to 4 days.

Bacon Waffles with Maple Cream

MAKES 9 TO 10 WAFFLES

Maple Cream

- 1 cup whipping cream
- ¼ cup maple syrup

Waffles

- 1 package (about 18 ounces) butter-recipe yellow cake mix
- 1¼ cups buttermilk*
- 3 eggs
- ½ cup (1 stick) butter, melted and cooled
- ¼ cup maple syrup
- 1 pound maple bacon, cooked and diced (about 1¾ cups)**

*If buttermilk is unavailable, substitute 3½ teaspoons vinegar or lemon juice and enough milk to equal 1¼ cups. Let stand 5 minutes.

**Also delicious with applewood-smoked bacon.

1. Preheat oven to 200°F. Place wire rack on top of baking sheet; place in oven. Preheat waffle maker according to manufacturer's directions. Spray cooking surface with nonstick cooking spray.

2. Beat whipping cream and ¼ cup syrup in chilled medium bowl with electric mixer at medium speed until soft peaks form. Refrigerate until ready to serve.

3. Combine cake mix, buttermilk, eggs, butter and ¼ cup syrup in large bowl. Add bacon; mix well. Spoon batter by ½ cupfuls onto heated waffle maker (batter will be thick). Cook 4 minutes or until steaming stops and waffles are lightly browned. Remove to wire rack in oven to keep warm. Repeat with remaining batter. Serve with chilled Maple Cream.

Waffled Breakfast Hash

MAKES 4 SERVINGS

1¼ pounds russet potatoes, peeled and cut into ½-inch pieces

½ small red onion, finely diced

1 small red bell pepper, cut into ½-inch pieces

⅓ cup sliced green onions, cut thinly on the bias

2 tablespoons vegetable oil

1 egg, lightly beaten

2 teaspoons cornstarch

½ teaspoon kosher salt

¼ teaspoon black pepper

4 fried eggs, for serving

1. Preheat classic waffle maker to medium-high heat. Set wire rack on large baking sheet.

2. Place potatoes in large saucepan filled with enough water to cover potatoes by 1 inch. Heat to a boil over high heat; reduce heat to medium-low and simmer, partially covered, about 6 to 8 minutes or until tender. Drain potatoes in colander; rinse with cold running water.

3. Place potatoes, onion, bell pepper, green onions, oil, beaten egg, cornstarch, salt and black pepper in large bowl; mix to combine.

4. Place 1 cup potato mixture in center of waffle maker. Close lid firmly; cook 5 minutes or until waffle is golden brown and crisp. Remove to wire rack; tent with foil to keep warm. Repeat with remaining potato mixture.

5. Serve hash with fried eggs.

Rich and Gooey Cinnamon Buns

MAKES 12 BUNS

Dough

- 1 package (¼ ounce) active dry yeast
- 1 cup warm milk (110°F)
- 2 eggs, beaten
- ½ cup granulated sugar
- ¼ cup (½ stick) butter, softened
- 1 teaspoon salt
- 4 to 4¼ cups all-purpose flour

Filling

- 1 cup packed brown sugar
- 3 tablespoons ground cinnamon
- Pinch of salt
- 6 tablespoons (¾ stick) butter, softened

Icing

- 1½ cups powdered sugar
- 3 ounces cream cheese, softened
- ¼ cup (½ stick) butter, softened
- ½ teaspoon vanilla
- ⅛ teaspoon salt

1. Dissolve yeast in warm milk in large bowl of electric mixer. Add eggs, granulated sugar, ¼ cup butter and 1 teaspoon salt; beat at medium speed 3 minutes or until well blended. Add 4 cups flour; beat at low speed until dough begins to come together. Knead dough with dough hook at low speed about 5 minutes or until smooth, elastic and slightly sticky, adding additional flour, 1 tablespoon at a time, if necessary to prevent sticking.

2. Shape dough into a ball. Place in large greased bowl; turn to grease top. Cover and let rise in warm place about 1 hour or until doubled in size. Meanwhile, for filling, combine brown sugar, cinnamon and pinch of salt in small bowl; mix well.

3. Spray 13×9-inch baking pan with nonstick cooking spray. Roll out dough into 18×14-inch rectangle on floured surface. Spread 6 tablespoons butter evenly over dough; top with cinnamon-sugar mixture. Beginning with long side, roll up dough tightly jelly-roll style; pinch seam to seal. Cut log crosswise into 12 slices; place slices cut sides up in prepared pan. Cover; let rise in warm place about 30 minutes or until almost doubled in size. Preheat oven to 350°F.

4. Bake 20 to 25 minutes or until golden brown. Meanwhile, for icing, combine powdered sugar, cream cheese, ¼ cup butter, vanilla and ⅛ teaspoon salt in medium bowl; beat with electric mixer at medium speed 2 minutes or until smooth and creamy. Spread icing generously over warm cinnamon buns.

Roasted Pepper and Sourdough Egg Dish

MAKES 6 SERVINGS

3 cups sourdough bread cubes

1 jar (12 ounces) roasted red pepper strips, drained

1 cup (4 ounces) shredded Monterey Jack cheese

1 cup (4 ounces) shredded sharp Cheddar cheese

1 cup cottage cheese

6 eggs

1 cup milk

¼ cup chopped fresh cilantro

¼ teaspoon black pepper

Slow Cooker Directions

1. Coat inside of slow cooker with nonstick cooking spray. Add bread cubes. Arrange roasted peppers evenly over bread cubes; sprinkle with Monterey Jack and Cheddar cheeses.

2. Place cottage cheese in food processor or blender; process until smooth. Add eggs and milk; process just until blended. Stir in cilantro and black pepper.

3. Pour egg mixture into slow cooker. Cover; cook on LOW 3 to 3½ hours or on HIGH 2 to 2½ hours or until eggs are firm but still moist.

Slurp-A-Soup

Chicken and Homemade Noodle Soup

MAKES 4 SERVINGS

¾ cup all-purpose flour, plus additional for work surface

2 teaspoons finely chopped fresh thyme, divided

¼ teaspoon salt

1 egg yolk, beaten

2 cups plus 3 tablespoons cold water, divided

1 pound boneless skinless chicken thighs, cut into ½- to ¾-inch pieces

5 cups chicken broth

1 onion, chopped

1 carrot, thinly sliced

¾ cup frozen peas

Chopped fresh Italian parsley

1. For noodles, combine ¾ cup flour, 1 teaspoon thyme and salt in a small bowl. Stir in egg yolk and 3 tablespoons water until well blended. Shape into a small ball. Place dough on lightly floured surface; flatten slightly. Knead 5 minutes or until dough is smooth and elastic, adding more flour to prevent sticking if necessary. Cover with plastic wrap. Let stand 15 minutes.

2. Roll out dough to ⅛-inch thickness or thinner on lightly floured surface. If dough is too elastic, let rest several minutes. Let dough rest about 30 minutes to dry slightly. Cut into ¼-inch-wide strips. Cut strips 1½ to 2 inches long; set aside.

3. Combine chicken and remaining 2 cups water in medium saucepan. Bring to a boil over high heat. Reduce heat to medium-low; cover and simmer 5 minutes or until chicken is cooked through. Drain chicken.

4. Combine broth, onion, carrot and remaining 1 teaspoon thyme in Dutch oven or large saucepan. Bring to a boil over high heat. Add noodles. Reduce heat to medium-low; simmer, uncovered, 8 minutes or until noodles are tender. Stir in chicken and peas; bring to a boil. Sprinkle with parsley.

Middle Eastern Lentil Soup

MAKES 4 SERVINGS

1 cup dried lentils

2 tablespoons olive oil

1 small onion, chopped

1 medium red bell pepper, chopped

1 teaspoon whole fennel seeds

½ teaspoon ground cumin

¼ teaspoon ground red pepper

4 cups water

½ teaspoon salt

1 tablespoon lemon juice

½ cup plain yogurt

2 tablespoons chopped fresh parsley

1. Rinse lentils, discarding any debris or blemished lentils; drain.

2. Heat oil in large saucepan over medium-high heat. Add onion and bell pepper; cook and stir 5 minutes or until tender. Add fennel seeds, cumin and ground red pepper; cook and stir 1 minute.

3. Add water, lentils and salt. Bring to a boil. Reduce heat to low. Cover; simmer 25 to 30 minutes or until lentils are tender. Stir in lemon juice.

4. To serve, ladle soup into individual bowls and top with yogurt; sprinkle with parsley.

Tip: Serve with homemade pita chips. Cut 4 pita bread rounds into six wedges each. Toss wedges with 1 tablespoon olive oil and 1 teaspoon coarse salt; spread on large baking sheet. Bake at 350°F 15 minutes or until light brown and crisp.

Beef Fajita Soup

MAKES 8 SERVINGS

1 pound cubed beef stew meat

1 can (about 15 ounces) pinto beans, rinsed and drained

1 can (about 15 ounces) black beans, rinsed and drained

1 can (about 14 ounces) diced tomatoes with roasted garlic

1 can (about 14 ounces) beef broth

1½ cups water

1 green bell pepper, thinly sliced

1 red bell pepper, thinly sliced

1 onion, thinly sliced

2 teaspoons ground cumin

1 teaspoon seasoned salt

1 teaspoon black pepper

Optional toppings: sour cream, shredded Monterey Jack or Cheddar cheese and/ or chopped olives

Slow Cooker Directions

1. Combine beef, beans, tomatoes, broth, water, bell peppers, onion, cumin, seasoned salt and black pepper in slow cooker.

2. Cover; cook on LOW 8 hours. Top as desired.

Roasted Tomato-Basil Soup

MAKES 6 SERVINGS

2 cans (28 ounces each) whole tomatoes, drained and juice reserved (about 3 cups juice)

2½ tablespoons packed dark brown sugar

1 onion, finely chopped

3 cups chicken broth

3 tablespoons tomato paste

¼ teaspoon ground allspice

1 can (5 ounces) evaporated milk

¼ cup chopped fresh basil

Salt and black pepper

Sprigs fresh basil (optional)

Onion slices (optional)

Slow Cooker Directions

1. Preheat oven to 450°F. Line baking sheet with foil; spray with nonstick cooking spray. Arrange tomatoes on foil in single layer. Sprinkle with brown sugar; top with chopped onion. Bake 25 to 30 minutes or until tomatoes look dry and are lightly browned. Let tomatoes cool slightly; finely chop.

2. Place tomato mixture, 3 cups reserved juice from tomatoes, broth, tomato paste and allspice in slow cooker; mix well. Cover; cook on LOW 8 hours or on HIGH 4 hours.

3. Add evaporated milk and basil; season with salt and pepper. Cover; cook on HIGH 30 minutes or until heated through. Garnish with basil and onion slices.

Cream of Broccoli Soup

MAKES 8 SERVINGS

1 bunch broccoli (about 1½ pounds), plus additional for garnish

3 cups canned chicken broth

1 medium onion, chopped

1 carrot, chopped

1 stalk celery, chopped

1 potato, peeled and chopped

1 clove garlic, minced

½ teaspoon dried basil

2 tablespoons butter

2 tablespoons all-purpose flour

1½ cups milk

1 cup half-and-half

½ teaspoon salt

¼ teaspoon black pepper

½ cup (2 ounces) shredded Cheddar cheese, plus additional for garnish

1. Trim leaves and ends from broccoli stalks. Peel stalks. Cut broccoli into ½-inch pieces.

2. Combine broth, onion, carrot, celery, potato, garlic and basil in large saucepan. Bring to a boil over high heat. Reduce heat to low; simmer 10 minutes. Add 1 bunch broccoli to saucepan. Simmer 10 minutes or until vegetables are fork-tender. Cool at room temperature 20 to 30 minutes. *Do not drain.*

3. Process vegetables in small batches in food processor or blender until smooth.

4. Melt butter in Dutch oven over medium heat. Add flour, stirring until mixture is smooth. Cook 1 minute. Gradually whisk in milk and half-and-half. Stir in salt, pepper and ½ cup cheese. Add puréed vegetables. Cook 3 to 5 minutes until mixture thickens, stirring occasionally.

5. Ladle soup into bowls. Garnish with additional broccoli and cheese.

French Onion Soup

MAKES 4 SERVINGS

4 tablespoons butter

1 package (3 ounces) ramen noodles, any flavor, broken into small pieces*

4 sweet yellow onions (about 2 pounds), thinly sliced

2 teaspoons sugar

1 teaspoon all-purpose flour

½ teaspoon salt

¼ teaspoon black pepper

1 cup dry white wine

2 cans (about 14 ounces each) beef broth

1 (8-inch) loaf French bread, sliced into 8 rounds

1 cup (about 4 ounces) shredded fontina cheese

*Discard seasoning packet.

1. Melt butter in large saucepan over medium heat. Add noodles; cook and stir 2 to 3 minutes or until golden. Add onions; cook 20 to 25 minutes or until golden and translucent, stirring occasionally.

2. Combine sugar, flour, salt and pepper in small bowl; add to noodle mixture. Add wine. Cook 3 minutes or until wine evaporates, stirring to scrape up browned bits. Add broth; bring to a boil. Reduce heat and simmer, partially covered, 10 minutes.

3. Preheat oven to 450°F. Line baking sheet with foil. Toast bread slices 5 minutes or until lightly browned. Sprinkle toast evenly with cheese; bake 3 minutes or until melted. Divide soup into bowls; top each with 2 slices toast. Serve immediately.

Note: If you have four individual heatproof bowls, the toast can be baked directly on top of the soup.

Hearty Beefy Beer Soup

MAKES 6 SERVINGS

1 tablespoon vegetable oil

¾ pound boneless beef round steak, cut into ½-inch pieces

1 large onion, chopped

2 medium carrots, sliced

2 stalks celery, diced

5 cups beef broth

1 bottle (12 ounces) stout or dark ale

¾ teaspoon dried oregano

¼ teaspoon salt

⅛ teaspoon black pepper

1 can (about 15 ounces) kidney beans, rinsed and drained

1 small zucchini, cut into ½-inch cubes

4 ounces mushrooms, sliced

1. Heat oil in 5-quart Dutch oven over medium heat. Add beef, onion, carrots and celery; cook and stir 6 to 8 minutes or until beef is no longer pink and carrots and celery are crisp-tender.

2. Stir in broth, stout, oregano, salt and pepper. Bring to a boil over high heat. Reduce heat to medium-low; simmer, uncovered, 45 minutes or until beef is fork-tender.

3. Stir beans, zucchini and mushrooms into soup. Bring to a boil over high heat. Reduce heat to medium-low; simmer, uncovered, 5 minutes or until zucchini is tender. Ladle into bowls.

Shortcut Chicken Tortilla Soup

MAKES 6 SERVINGS

2 cans (about 14 ounces each) chicken broth

4 boneless skinless chicken breasts (about 1 pound)

2 jars (16 ounces each) corn and black bean salsa

3 tablespoons vegetable oil

1 tablespoon taco seasoning mix

1 package (3 ounces) ramen noodles, any flavor, broken into small pieces*

4 ounces Monterey Jack cheese, grated

Discard seasoning packet.

1. Bring broth to a simmer in large saucepan. Add chicken; cook 12 to 15 minutes or until no longer pink in center. Remove chicken to large cutting board; set aside until cool enough to handle. Shred chicken with two forks.

2. Add salsa to saucepan; cook 5 minutes or until soup comes to a simmer. Return shredded chicken to saucepan; cook 5 minutes until thoroughly heated through.

3. Combine oil and taco seasoning mix in small bowl. Add noodles; toss to coat. Cook and stir noodles in medium skillet over medium heat 8 to 10 minutes or until toasted. Top soup with toasted noodles and grated cheese.

Serving Suggestions: Serve soup with lime wedges, chopped avocado or fresh cilantro.

Hearty Mushroom Barley Soup

MAKES 4 SERVINGS

Nonstick cooking spray

1 teaspoon extra virgin olive oil

2 cups chopped onions

1 cup thinly sliced carrots

2 cans (about 14 ounces each) chicken broth

12 ounces sliced mushrooms

1 can (10¾ ounces) cream of mushroom soup, undiluted

½ cup uncooked quick-cooking barley

1 teaspoon Worcestershire sauce

½ teaspoon dried thyme

¼ cup finely chopped green onions

¼ teaspoon salt

¼ teaspoon black pepper

1. Coat Dutch oven or large saucepan with cooking spray; heat over medium-high heat. Add oil; tilt pan to coat bottom of pan. Add onions; cook and stir 8 minutes or until onions just begin to turn golden. Add carrots; cook and stir 2 minutes.

2. Add broth, mushrooms, soup, barley, Worcestershire sauce and thyme; bring to a boil over high heat. Reduce heat; cover and simmer 15 minutes, stirring occasionally. Stir in green onions, salt and pepper.

Potato Cheddar Soup

MAKES 6 SERVINGS

2 pounds new red potatoes, cut into ½-inch cubes

3 cups chicken or vegetable broth

¾ cup coarsely chopped carrots

1 medium onion, coarsely chopped

½ teaspoon salt

1 cup half-and-half

¼ teaspoon black pepper

2 cups (8 ounces) shredded Cheddar cheese

Slow Cooker Directions

1. Place potatoes, broth, carrots, onion and salt in slow cooker. Cover; cook on LOW 6 to 7 hours or on HIGH 3 to 4 hours.

2. Stir in half-and-half and pepper. Cover; cook on HIGH 15 minutes. Turn off heat. Let stand, uncovered, 5 minutes. Stir in cheese until melted.

Fresh Lime and Black Bean Soup

MAKES 4 SERVINGS

- 2 cans (about 15 ounces each) black beans, undrained
- 1 can (about 14 ounces) chicken broth
- 1½ cups chopped onions
- 1½ teaspoons chili powder
- ¾ teaspoon ground cumin
- ¼ teaspoon garlic powder
- ⅛ to ¼ teaspoon red pepper flakes
- ½ cup sour cream
- 2 tablespoons extra virgin olive oil
- 2 tablespoons chopped fresh cilantro
- 1 lime, cut into wedges

Slow Cooker Directions

1. Coat inside of slow cooker with nonstick cooking spray. Add beans, broth, onions, chili powder, cumin, garlic powder and red pepper flakes. Cover; cook on LOW 7 hours or on HIGH 3½ hours or until onions are very soft.

2. To thicken soup, place half of soup mixture in food processor or blender; process until smooth. Stir into remaining soup in slow cooker. Turn off heat. Let stand 15 to 20 minutes before serving.

3. Serve soup with sour cream, oil, cilantro and lime wedges.

Hoppin' John Soup

MAKES 6 SERVINGS

- 1 bag SUCCESS® Brown Rice
- ¼ pound spicy turkey sausage
- ½ pound turnips, peeled and chopped
- ½ cup chopped onion
- 2 carrots, peeled and chopped
- ½ teaspoon salt
- ½ teaspoon black pepper
- 3 cups chicken broth
- 1 package (8 ounces) frozen black-eyed peas, thawed and drained
- 1 package (8 ounces) frozen chopped mustard greens, thawed and drained
- ½ teaspoon red pepper flakes

Prepare rice according to package directions.

Brown sausage in large saucepan or Dutch oven over medium-high heat; drain. Add turnips, onion, carrots, salt and pepper. Reduce heat to low; simmer 7 minutes. Add broth; simmer 5 minutes. Add rice, peas and greens; simmer 10 minutes, stirring occasionally. Sprinkle with red pepper flakes.

Hot Gazpacho Bean Soup

MAKES 6 SERVINGS

1 tablespoon olive oil

1 cup chopped onion

1 cup chopped green
   bell pepper

1 clove garlic, minced

2 cans (11½ ounces
   each) vegetable
   juice

1 can (about 15 ounces)
   red kidney beans,
   rinsed and drained

1 can (about 15 ounces)
   chickpeas, rinsed
   and drained

2 cubes beef bouillon

2 tablespoons fresh
   lemon juice

¼ teaspoon red pepper
   flakes

3 cups chopped
   tomatoes, divided

1 cup chopped
   cucumber

½ cup chopped green
   onions

½ cup plain salad
   croutons

1. Heat oil in medium saucepan over medium-high heat. Add onion, bell pepper and garlic; cook 3 minutes or until vegetables are crisp-tender.

2. Add vegetable juice, beans, chickpeas, bouillon cubes, lemon juice, red pepper flakes and 1½ cups tomatoes. Bring to a boil. Reduce heat to low. Cover and simmer 5 minutes.

3. Divide bean mixture among serving bowls. Top with remaining tomatoes, cucumber, green onions and croutons.

Hearty Vegetable Pasta Soup

MAKES 6 SERVINGS

1 tablespoon vegetable oil

1 onion, chopped

3 cups vegetable broth

1 can (about 14 ounces) diced tomatoes

1 medium potato, cubed

2 carrots, sliced

1 stalk celery, sliced

1 teaspoon dried basil

½ teaspoon salt

⅛ teaspoon black pepper

⅓ cup uncooked tiny bowtie pasta

2 ounces fresh spinach, stemmed and chopped

1. Heat oil in Dutch oven over medium-high heat. Add onion; cook and stir 6 minutes or until onion is translucent. Add broth, tomatoes, potato, carrots, celery, basil, salt and pepper; bring to a boil over high heat. Reduce heat to medium-low; simmer, uncovered, 20 minutes or until potato and carrots are very tender, stirring occasionally.

2. Stir in pasta; simmer, uncovered, 8 minutes or until pasta is tender.

3. Stir spinach into soup. Simmer, uncovered, 2 minutes or until spinach is wilted. Serve immediately.

Italian-Style Bean Soup

MAKES 8 TO 10 SERVINGS

1½ cups dried Great Northern or navy beans, rinsed and sorted

5 to 6 cups water

1 cup pasta sauce

1 tablespoon minced onion

2 teaspoons dried basil

2 cubes chicken bouillon

1 teaspoon dried parsley flakes

½ teaspoon minced fresh garlic

1½ cups uncooked medium pasta shells

8 ounces baby spinach leaves (optional)

Salt and black pepper

¼ cup grated Parmesan cheese

1. Place beans in large bowl; cover with water. Soak 6 to 8 hours or overnight.*

2. Drain beans; discard water. Combine soaked beans, 5 cups water, pasta sauce, onion, basil, bouillon cubes, parsley flakes and garlic in Dutch oven; bring to a boil over high heat. Cover; reduce heat and simmer 2 to 2½ hours.

3. Add pasta and spinach, if desired; cover and simmer 15 to 20 minutes or until pasta is tender. Season with salt and pepper. Top with cheese.

*To quick soak beans, place in large saucepan; cover with water. Bring to a boil over high heat; boil 2 minutes. Remove from heat; let soak, covered, 1 hour.

Variations: Add 8 slices crisp-cooked bacon, crumbled *or* 1 package (15 ounces) frozen precooked Italian style meatballs, not in sauce.

Feed the
Beast-wiches

Smoked Ham, Swiss & Caramelized Onion Sandwich

MAKES 1 SERVING

- 1 tablespoon HELLMANN'S® or BEST FOODS® Real Mayonnaise
- 1 multigrain Kaiser roll
- 2 thin slices deli smoked ham (about 2 ounces)
- 2 thin slices Swiss cheese (about 2 ounces)

  Caramelized onions (recipe follows)
- 2 slices tomato (optional)
- 1 green leaf lettuce leaf

Evenly spread HELLMANN'S® or BEST FOODS® Real Mayonnaise on roll, then top with remaining ingredients.

Caramelized Onions: Melt 2 tablespoons COUNTRY CROCK® Spread in 10-inch nonstick skillet over medium-high heat. Cook 1 thinly sliced medium onion, stirring occasionally, until dark golden brown and very tender, about 10 minutes.

Spicy Meatball Sandwiches

MAKES 6 SANDWICHES

1 large (17×15-inch) foil cooking bag

1 jar (26 ounces) marinara sauce

1 pound frozen precooked Italian-style meatballs

½ cup chopped green bell pepper

⅓ cup sliced black olives

2 teaspoons Italian seasoning

¼ teaspoon ground red pepper

6 slices mozzarella cheese, halved lengthwise

6 hoagie buns

3 tablespoons finely shredded Parmesan cheese

1. Prepare grill for direct cooking.

2. Place bag on baking sheet. Combine marinara sauce, meatballs, bell pepper, olives, Italian seasoning and ground red pepper in large bowl. Pour into bag. Double fold open side of bag, leaving head space for heat circulation.

3. Slide bag off baking sheet onto grill grid. Grill, covered, over medium-high coals 11 to 13 minutes or until meatballs are heated through. Carefully open bag to allow steam to escape.

4. Meanwhile, place 2 pieces mozzarella cheese on bottom of each bun. Spoon meatball mixture onto buns. Sprinkle with Parmesan cheese.

Western Barbecue Burgers with Beer Barbecue Sauce

MAKES 4 SERVINGS

1½ pounds ground beef

1 cup smokehouse-style barbecue sauce

¼ cup brown ale

½ teaspoon salt

¼ teaspoon black pepper

1 red onion, cut into ½-inch-thick slices

4 hamburger buns

8 slices thick-cut bacon, crisp-cooked

Lettuce leaves

Tomato slices

1. Prepare grill for direct cooking over medium-high heat. Shape beef into four patties about ¾ inch thick.

2. Combine barbecue sauce, ale, salt and pepper in small saucepan. Bring to a boil; boil 1 minute. Set aside.

3. Grill burgers, covered, 8 to 10 minutes or to desired doneness, turning occasionally. Grill onion 4 minutes or until softened and slightly charred, turning occasionally.

4. Serve burgers on buns topped with onion, bacon, barbecue sauce mixture, lettuce and tomatoes.

Bacon & Tomato Melts

MAKES 4 SANDWICHES

8 slices bacon, crisp-
 cooked

8 slices (1 ounce each)
 Cheddar cheese

2 tomatoes, sliced

8 slices whole wheat
 bread

¼ cup (½ stick) butter,
 melted

1. Layer 2 slices bacon, 2 slices cheese and tomato slices on each of 4 bread slices; top with remaining bread slices. Brush sandwiches with butter.

2. Heat grill pan or large skillet over medium heat. Add sandwiches; press lightly with spatula or weigh down with small plate. Cook 4 to 5 minutes per side or until cheese melts and sandwiches are golden brown.

Southwestern Sloppy Joes

MAKES 9 SERVINGS

1 pound ground beef

1 cup chopped onion

¼ cup chopped celery

¼ cup water

1 can (10 ounces) diced tomatoes with mild green chiles

1 can (8 ounces) tomato sauce

4 teaspoons packed brown sugar

½ teaspoon ground cumin

¼ teaspoon salt

9 whole wheat hamburger buns

1. Heat large nonstick skillet over medium-high heat. Add beef, onion, celery and water; cook and stir 6 to 8 minutes, stirring to break up meat. Drain fat.

2. Stir in tomatoes, tomato sauce, brown sugar, cumin and salt; bring to a boil over high heat. Reduce heat to low; cook 20 minutes or until mixture thickens. Spoon ⅓ cup meat mixture onto each bun.

Stuffed Focaccia Sandwiches

MAKES 4 SANDWICHES

1 container (about 5 ounces) soft cheese with garlic and herbs

1 (10-inch) round herb or onion focaccia, cut in half horizontally

½ cup thinly sliced red onion

½ cup coarsely chopped pimiento-stuffed green olives, drained

¼ cup sliced mild banana pepper

4 ounces thinly sliced deli hard salami

6 ounces thinly sliced oven-roasted turkey breast

1 package (⅔ ounce) fresh basil, stems removed

1. Spread soft cheese over cut sides of focaccia. Layer bottom half evenly with onion, olives, pepper, salami, turkey and basil. Cover sandwich with top half of focaccia; press down firmly.

2. Cut sandwich into four equal pieces. Serve immediately or wrap individually in plastic wrap and refrigerate until serving time.

Tip: This sandwich is great for make-ahead lunches or picnics.

Pulled Pork Sandwiches

MAKES 6 TO 8 SERVINGS

2 tablespoons kosher salt

2 tablespoons packed light brown sugar

2 tablespoons paprika

1 teaspoon dry mustard

1 teaspoon black pepper

1 boneless pork shoulder roast (about 3 pounds)

1½ cups stout

½ cup cider vinegar

6 to 8 large hamburger buns, split

¾ cup barbecue sauce

1. Preheat oven to 325°F. Combine salt, brown sugar, paprika, dry mustard and pepper in small bowl; mix well. Rub into pork.

2. Place pork in 4-quart Dutch oven. Add stout and vinegar. Cover; bake 3 hours or until meat is fork-tender. Cool 15 to 30 minutes or until cool enough to handle.

3. Shred pork with two forks. Divide onto buns and serve warm with barbecue sauce.

Tip: This recipe is a great dish for a picnic or party. Baked beans, corn on the cob and watermelon are wonderful accompaniments.

Cheddar Stuffed Beef Burgers

MAKES 4 SERVINGS

Nonstick cooking spray

2 large baking potatoes, washed and dried

12 ounces ground sirloin

½ teaspoon dried thyme

4 slices sharp Cheddar cheese

⅛ cup water

4 slices beefsteak tomato

4 romaine lettuce leaves

1. Preheat oven to 450°F. Spray large baking sheet with cooking spray. Cut each potato crosswise into 8 round slices. Place slices on baking sheet. Bake 25 to 30 minutes or until lightly browned.

2. Mix ground sirloin and thyme in mixing bowl. Form into eight balls. Fold each slice of cheese in half four times, forming a cube.

3. Press cheese cube in between two ground sirloin balls, sealing cheese inside. Form into patty by flattening to approximately 1½ inch thick. Repeat for three more patties.

4. Lightly coat deep skillet with cooking spray. Heat skillet over medium-high heat. Add stuffed patties; cook 3 minutes on each side. Add water; cover and cook 6 minutes.

5. Place each burger on slice of potato. Top with tomato slice, lettuce leaf and another slice of potato.

Diner Egg Salad Sandwiches

MAKES 4 SERVINGS

6 eggs

2 tablespoons mayonnaise

1½ tablespoons sweet pickle relish

½ cup finely chopped celery

⅛ to ¼ teaspoon salt

Black pepper (optional)

8 slices whole grain bread

1. Place eggs in medium saucepan; add cold water to cover. Bring to a boil over high heat. Immediately reduce heat to low; simmer 10 minutes. Drain and peel eggs under cold running water.

2. Cut eggs in half. Discard 4 yolk halves or reserve for another use. Set aside all 6 egg whites. Place reserved egg yolks in medium bowl. Add mayonnaise and pickle relish; mash with fork until yolk mixture is well blended and creamy.

3. Chop egg whites. Add egg whites, celery and salt to yolk mixture; stir until well blended. Season with pepper, if desired. Spread ½ cup egg salad on each of 4 bread slices; top with remaining bread slices. Slice sandwiches in half, if desired, before serving.

Grilled Chicken Sandwiches with Basil Spread with Real Mayonnaise

MAKES 4 SERVINGS

⅓ cup HELLMANN'S® or BEST FOODS® Real Mayonnaise

¼ cup finely chopped fresh basil leaves

¼ cup grated Parmesan cheese

8 slices whole-grain bread

1 pound boneless, skinless chicken breast halves, grilled and sliced

8 slices tomato (optional)

4 slices bacon, crisp-cooked and halved crosswise

Combine HELLMANN'S® or BEST FOODS® Real Mayonnaise, basil and cheese in small bowl. Evenly spread mixture on bread slices. Equally top 4 bread slices with chicken, tomato, if desired, and bacon, then top with remaining bread.

Philly Cheesesteak Hero Sandwiches

MAKES 4 SERVINGS

1 tablespoon vegetable oil

1 large onion, thinly sliced (about 1 cup)

1 medium green **or** red bell pepper, cut thinly into 2-inch-long slices (about 1½ cups)

1 pound thinly sliced beef sirloin steak **or** 8 frozen sandwich steaks (about 2 ounces **each**)

1 jar (14.5 ounces) PREGO® Creamy Cheddar Cheese Sauce

4 (8-inch) long hard rolls, split

1. Heat the oil in a 12-inch skillet over medium-high heat. Add the onion and pepper; cook for 15 minutes or until the vegetables are tender, stirring occasionally. Remove the vegetables from the skillet and set aside.

2. Add **half** of the steak to the skillet and cook for 2 to 3 minutes or until the steak is cooked through, stirring occasionally. Remove the steak from the skillet and keep warm. Repeat with the remaining steak.

3. Return the vegetables to the skillet and stir in the cheese sauce. Heat over medium heat until heated through, stirring occasionally.

4. Divide the steak evenly among the rolls and top **each** with ½ **cup** of the vegetable mixture. Serve immediately.

Havarti & Onion Sandwiches

MAKES 2 SANDWICHES

- 1½ teaspoons olive oil
- ⅓ cup thinly sliced red onion
- 4 slices pumpernickel bread
- 6 ounces dill havarti cheese, cut into slices
- ½ cup prepared coleslaw

1. Heat oil in large skillet over medium heat. Add onion; cook and stir 5 minutes or until tender. Layer 2 bread slices with onion, cheese and coleslaw; top with remaining 2 bread slices.

2. Heat same grill pan over medium heat. Add sandwiches; press down with spatula or weigh down with small plate. Cook 4 to 5 minutes on each side or until cheese melts and sandwiches are browned.

Sweet 'n' Spicy Barbecued Brisket Sandwiches

MAKES 10 SERVINGS

1 trimmed beef brisket (about 5 pounds)

Ground black pepper

1 tablespoon garlic powder

2 cups PACE® Picante Sauce

½ cup packed brown sugar

½ cup Worcestershire sauce

10 PEPPERIDGE FARM® Classic Sandwich Buns with Sesame Seeds

1. Season the beef with the black pepper and garlic powder and place into a 3-quart shallow baking dish. Stir the picante sauce, brown sugar and Worcestershire in a small bowl. Spread the picante sauce mixture over the beef. Cover and refrigerate overnight.

2. Bake, covered, at 300°F. for 4½ to 5 hours or until the beef is fork-tender. Slice or shred the beef and serve with the juices on the rolls.

Bacon and Cheese Rarebit

MAKES 6 SERVINGS

1½ tablespoons butter

½ cup lager (not dark beer)

2 teaspoons Worcestershire sauce

2 teaspoons Dijon mustard

⅛ teaspoon ground red pepper

2 cups (8 ounces) shredded American cheese

1½ cups (6 ounces) shredded sharp Cheddar cheese

1 small loaf (8 ounces) egg bread or challah, cut into 6 (1-inch-thick) slices

12 large slices tomato

12 slices bacon, crisp-cooked

1. Preheat broiler. Line medium baking sheet with foil.

2. Melt butter in double boiler set over simmering water. Stir in lager, Worcestershire sauce, mustard and ground red pepper; cook until heated through, stirring occasionally. Gradually add cheeses, stirring constantly until melted. Remove from heat; cover and keep warm.

3. Broil bread slices until golden brown. Arrange on prepared baking sheet. Top each serving with tomato and bacon. Spoon about ¼ cup cheese sauce evenly over each serving. Broil 4 to 5 inches from heat just until cheese sauce begins to brown.

Parmesan Honey Lager Burgers

MAKES 4 SERVINGS

1½ pounds ground beef

¾ cup honey lager, divided

⅓ cup grated Parmesan cheese

1 tablespoon Worcestershire sauce

¼ teaspoon black pepper

3 tablespoons mayonnaise

3 tablespoons ketchup

½ teaspoon yellow mustard

4 Kaiser rolls

8 slices tomato

8 thin slices red onion

1. Lightly oil grid. Prepare grill for direct cooking over medium-high heat.

2. Combine beef, ¼ cup lager, cheese, Worcestershire sauce and pepper in large bowl; mix lightly. Shape into four patties. Combine 1 tablespoon lager, mayonnaise, ketchup and mustard in small bowl; set aside.

3. Grill burgers, turning and basting with remaining lager often, until at least 145°F or desired doneness.

4. Serve burgers on rolls with tomato slices, onion slices and mayonnaise mixture.

Chow Down
Meals

Fajita Pile-Ups

MAKES 4 SERVINGS

- 2 teaspoons vegetable oil, divided
- ¾ pound beef top sirloin steak, trimmed of fat, cut into thin strips
- 2 teaspoons steak seasoning
- ½ medium lime
- 1 medium green bell pepper, cut into ½-inch strips
- 1 medium red or yellow bell pepper, cut into ½-inch strips
- 1 large onion, cut into ½-inch wedges
- 1 cup cherry tomatoes, halved
- ½ teaspoon ground cumin
- 4 (6-inch) corn tortillas
- ½ cup sour cream
- 2 tablespoons chopped fresh cilantro (optional)
- Lime wedges (optional)

1. Heat 1 teaspoon oil in large nonstick skillet over medium-high heat. Add steak; sprinkle with steak seasoning. Cook and stir 3 minutes or just until slightly pink in center. *Do not overcook.* Remove to plate. Squeeze ½ lime over steak. Cover with foil to keep warm.

2. Add remaining 1 teaspoon oil to skillet. Add bell peppers and onion; cook and stir 8 minutes or just until tender. Add tomatoes; cook and stir 1 minute. Return steak with any accumulated juices and cumin to skillet; cook and stir 1 minute.

3. Warm tortillas according to package directions. Top tortillas evenly with steak mixture. Serve with sour cream; garnish with cilantro and lime wedges.

Spicy Buttermilk Oven-Fried Chicken

MAKES 6 SERVINGS

1 cut-up whole chicken (3½ pounds)

2 cups buttermilk

1½ cups all-purpose flour

1 teaspoon salt

1 teaspoon ground red pepper

½ teaspoon garlic powder

¼ cup canola oil

1. Place chicken pieces in single layer in 13×9-inch baking dish. Pour buttermilk over chicken. Cover with plastic wrap and refrigerate; let marinate at least 2 hours.

2. Preheat oven to 350°F. Combine flour, salt, ground red pepper and garlic powder in large shallow bowl. Heat oil in large skillet over medium-high heat.

3. Remove chicken pieces from buttermilk; coat with flour mixture. Place chicken in hot oil; cook about 10 minutes or until brown and crisp on all sides. Place chicken in single layer in 13×9-inch baking dish. Bake, uncovered, 30 to 45 minutes or until chicken is cooked through (165°F).

Lemon-Orange Glazed Ribs

MAKES 4 SERVINGS

3 pounds baby back pork ribs, cut into halves

2 tablespoons fresh lemon juice

2 tablespoons orange juice

2 tablespoons soy sauce

2 cloves garlic, minced

¼ cup orange marmalade

1 tablespoon hoisin sauce

1. Place ribs in large resealable food storage bag. Combine lemon and orange juices, soy sauce and garlic in small bowl; pour over ribs. Seal bag; turn to coat. Marinate in refrigerator at least 4 hours or up to 24 hours, turning once.

2. Preheat oven to 350°F. Drain ribs; reserve marinade. Place ribs on rack in shallow, foil-lined roasting pan. Brush half of marinade evenly over ribs; bake 20 minutes. Turn ribs over; brush with remaining marinade. Bake 20 minutes.

3. Remove ribs from oven; pour off drippings. Combine marmalade and hoisin sauce in cup; brush half of mixture over ribs. Return to oven; bake 10 minutes or until glazed. Turn ribs over; brush with remaining marmalade mixture. Bake 10 minutes or until ribs are browned and glazed.

Beer-Basted Barbecue Pork Chops

MAKES 6 SERVINGS

1 cup prepared barbecue sauce, divided

1 cup plus 3 tablespoons beer, divided

3 tablespoons honey

1 tablespoon chili powder

6 bone-in loin pork chops, cut about 1 inch thick

1 teaspoon salt

½ teaspoon black pepper

1. Combine ½ cup barbecue sauce, 1 cup beer, honey and chili powder in large bowl. Add pork chops, turning to coat; refrigerate 2 to 4 hours, turning occasionally. Combine remaining ½ cup barbecue sauce and 3 tablespoons beer in separate bowl; set aside.

2. Prepare grill for direct cooking over medium-high heat. Oil grid.

3. Remove pork chops from beer mixture and sprinkle with salt and pepper. Place pork chops on prepared grid over medium-high heat. Grill 4 minutes. Turn chops over; brush with half of reserved barbecue sauce mixture. Grill 3 minutes. Turn over; brush with remaining sauce mixture and grill 4 to 5 minutes or until an instant read thermometer inserted into the thickest portion of pork chops registers 150°F.

Greek Chicken & Spinach Rice Casserole

MAKES 4 SERVINGS

Nonstick cooking spray

1 cup finely chopped onion

1 package (10 ounces) frozen chopped spinach, thawed and squeezed dry

1 cup uncooked quick-cooking brown rice

1 cup water

¼ teaspoon salt

⅛ teaspoon ground red pepper

¾ pound chicken tenders

2 teaspoons Greek seasoning (oregano, rosemary and sage mixture)

½ teaspoon lemon-pepper seasoning

1 tablespoon olive oil

1 lemon, cut into wedges

1. Preheat oven to 350°F. Spray large ovenproof skillet with cooking spray; heat over medium heat. Add onion; cook and stir 2 minutes or until translucent. Add spinach, rice, water, salt and ground red pepper; stir until well blended. Remove from heat.

2. Place chicken on top of mixture in skillet in single layer. Sprinkle with Greek seasoning and lemon-pepper seasoning. Cover with foil. Bake 25 minutes or until chicken is no longer pink in center.

3. Remove foil. Drizzle oil evenly over top. Serve with lemon wedges.

Steak Parmesan

MAKES 2 TO 3 SERVINGS

4 cloves garlic, minced

1 tablespoon olive oil

1 tablespoon coarse salt

1 teaspoon chopped fresh rosemary

1 teaspoon black pepper

2 beef T-bone or Porterhouse steaks, cut 1 inch thick (about 2 pounds)

¼ cup grated Parmesan cheese

1. Prepare grill for direct cooking. Combine garlic, oil, salt, rosemary and pepper; press into both sides of steaks. Let stand 15 minutes.

2. Place steaks on grid over medium-high heat. Cover; grill 14 to 19 minutes or until internal temperature reaches 145°F for medium rare doneness, turning once.

3. Remove steaks to large cutting board; sprinkle with cheese. Tent with foil; let stand 5 minutes. Serve immediately.

Tip: For a smoky flavor, soak 2 cups hickory or oak wood chips in cold water to cover at least 30 minutes. Drain and scatter over hot coals before grilling. Makes 2 to 3 servings.

Garlic Pork with Roasted Red Potatoes

MAKES 4 SERVINGS

Nonstick cooking spray

½ teaspoon paprika

½ teaspoon garlic powder

1 pound pork tenderloin

1 tablespoon extra virgin olive oil

6 new red potatoes, scrubbed and quartered (12 ounces total)

1 teaspoon dried oregano

½ teaspoon salt

½ teaspoon black pepper

1. Preheat oven to 425°F. Spray 13×9-inch baking pan with cooking spray.

2. Combine paprika and garlic powder in small bowl; sprinkle evenly over pork.

3. Spray large skillet with cooking spray; heat over medium-high heat. Cook pork 3 minutes per side or until browned. Place in center of prepared pan.

4. Remove skillet from heat. Add oil, potatoes and oregano; toss to coat. Arrange potato mixture around pork, scraping up sides and bottom of skillet with rubber spatula. Combine salt and pepper in small bowl; sprinkle evenly over all. Bake, uncovered, 22 minutes or until pork reaches 155° to 160°F.

5. Remove pork to large cutting board; let stand 5 minutes before slicing. Stir potatoes; cover with foil and let stand while pork is resting. Serve pork with potatoes.

Broccoli and Brown Rice Casserole

MAKES 6 SERVINGS

- 1 tablespoon vegetable oil
- 8 ounces sliced mushrooms
- 1 cup onion, chopped
- 1 teaspoon garlic, chopped
- 2 tablespoons all-purpose flour
- 1 cup milk
- 2 cups cooked SUCCESS®, MAHATMA®, CAROLINA® or RICELAND® Whole Grain Brown Rice
- 1 cup shredded Cheddar cheese, divided
- 1 package (10 ounces) frozen chopped broccoli, thawed and drained
- 1½ teaspoons salt

Preheat oven to 375°F. Heat oil in a large skillet. Sauté mushrooms, onion and garlic for 5 minutes or until all liquid is absorbed. Sprinkle flour over mushroom mixture; stir. Stir in milk and bring to a boil, stirring frequently. Reduce heat and simmer for 2 minutes. Remove from heat and stir in rice, ¾ cup cheese, broccoli and salt. Mix well. Pour into a 2-quart casserole dish and top with remaining cheese. Cover with aluminum foil and bake for 10 minutes.

Tip: To create a main dish, stir in 2 cups diced, cooked chicken.

Honey Lemon Garlic Chicken

MAKES 4 SERVINGS

2 lemons, divided

2 tablespoons butter, melted

2 tablespoons honey

3 cloves garlic, chopped

2 sprigs fresh rosemary, leaves removed from stems

1 teaspoon coarse salt

½ teaspoon black pepper

3 pounds chicken (4 bone-in skin-on chicken thighs and 4 drumsticks)

1¼ pounds unpeeled small potatoes, cut into halves or quarters

1. Preheat oven to 375°F. Grate peel and squeeze juice from 1 lemon. Cut remaining lemon into slices.

2. Combine lemon peel, lemon juice, butter, honey, garlic, rosemary leaves, salt and pepper in small bowl; mix well. Combine chicken, potatoes and lemon slices in large bowl. Pour butter mixture over chicken and potatoes; toss to coat. Arrange in single layer on large rimmed baking sheet or in shallow roasting pan.

3. Bake 1 hour or until potatoes are tender and chicken is cooked through (165°F). Cover loosely with foil if chicken skin is becoming too dark.

Sage-Roasted Pork with Rutabaga

MAKES 4 TO 6 SERVINGS

1 bunch fresh sage

4 cloves garlic, minced (2 tablespoons)

1½ teaspoons coarse salt, divided

1 teaspoon coarsely ground black pepper, divided

5 tablespoons extra virgin olive oil, divided

1 boneless pork loin roast (2 to 2½ pounds)

2 medium or 1 large rutabaga (1 to 1½ pounds)

Nonstick cooking spray

4 carrots, cut into 1½-inch pieces

1. Chop enough sage to measure 2 tablespoons; reserve remaining sage. Mash chopped sage, garlic, ½ teaspoon salt and ½ teaspoon pepper in small bowl to form paste. Stir in 2 tablepoons oil.

2. Score fatty side of pork roast with sharp knife, making cuts about ¼ inch deep. Rub herb paste into cuts and over all sides of pork. Place pork on large plate; cover and refrigerate 1 to 2 hours.

3. Preheat oven to 400°F. Spray large roasting pan with cooking spray. Cut rutabaga into halves or quarters; peel and cut into 1½-inch pieces.* Combine rutabaga and carrots in large bowl. Drizzle with remaining 3 tablespoons oil and sprinkle with remaining 1 teaspoon salt and ½ teaspoon pepper; toss to coat.

4. Arrange vegetables in single layer in prepared pan. Place pork on top of vegetables, scraping up any remaining herb paste from plate into roasting pan. Tuck 3 sprigs of remaining sage into vegetables.

5. Roast 15 minutes. *Reduce oven temperature to 325°F.* Roast 45 minutes to 1 hour 15 minutes or until internal temperature reaches 145°F and pork is barely pink in center, stirring vegetables once or twice during cooking time. Let roast stand 5 minutes before slicing.

*Rutabagas can be difficult to cut—they are a tough vegetable and slippery on the outside because they are waxed. Cutting them into large pieces (halves or quarters) before peeling and chopping makes them easier to manage.

Onion-Crusted Meatloaf with Roasted Potatoes

MAKES 6 SERVINGS

---

1 can (10¾ ounces) CAMPBELL'S® Condensed Tomato Soup

1½ pounds ground beef

1 can (2.8 ounces) French fried onions

1 egg, beaten

1 tablespoon Worcestershire sauce

6 small potatoes, cut into quarters

1. Thoroughly mix ½ **cup** soup, beef, ½ **can** onions, egg and Worcestershire in a large bowl. Place the mixture in a 13×9×2-inch baking pan and firmly shape into an 8×4-inch loaf. Spoon the remaining soup over the meatloaf. Arrange the potatoes around the meatloaf.

2. Bake at 400°F. for 1 hour or until the meatloaf is cooked through. Stir the potatoes. Sprinkle the remaining onions over the meatloaf and bake for 3 minutes or until the onions are golden.

Grilled Chicken Tostadas

MAKES 4 SERVINGS

1 pound boneless skinless chicken breasts

1 teaspoon ground cumin

¼ cup orange juice

¼ cup plus 2 tablespoons salsa, divided

1 tablespoon plus 2 teaspoons vegetable oil, divided

2 cloves garlic, minced

8 green onions

1 can (16 ounces) refried beans

4 (10-inch) *or* 8 (6- to 7-inch) flour tortillas

2 cups chopped romaine lettuce

1½ cups (6 ounces) shredded Monterey Jack cheese with jalapeño peppers

1 medium ripe avocado, diced (optional)

1 medium tomato, seeded and diced (optional)

Chopped fresh cilantro and sour cream (optional)

1. Place chicken in single layer in shallow glass dish; sprinkle with cumin. Combine orange juice, ¼ cup salsa, 1 tablespoon oil and garlic in small bowl; pour over chicken. Cover; marinate in refrigerator at least 2 hours or up to 8 hours, stirring occasionally.

2. Prepare grill for direct cooking.

3. Drain chicken; reserve marinade. Brush green onions with remaining 2 teaspoons oil. Grill chicken and green onions, covered, over medium-high heat 5 minutes. Brush tops of chicken with half of reserved marinade; turn and brush with remaining marinade. Turn green onions; grill, covered, 5 minutes or until chicken is no longer pink in center and green onions are tender.

4. Meanwhile, combine beans and remaining 2 tablespoons salsa in small saucepan; cook 15 minutes over medium heat until heated through, stirring occasionally.

5. Place tortillas in single layer on grid. Grill, uncovered, 1 to 2 minutes per side or until golden brown. (Pierce any tortillas which puff up with tip of knife.)

6. Remove chicken and green onions to large cutting board. Slice chicken crosswise into ½-inch strips. Cut green onions crosswise into 1-inch pieces. Spread bean mixture over tortillas; top with lettuce, chicken, green onions, cheese, avocado and tomato, if desired. Sprinkle with cilantro and serve with sour cream, if desired.

Texas Smoked BBQ Brisket

MAKES 10 TO 12 SERVINGS

½ cup prepared barbecue seasoning

2 tablespoons ground chili powder

1 (5- to 7-pound) beef brisket, trimmed with a layer of fat (center flat portion)

1 cup FRANK'S® RedHot® Original Cayenne Pepper Sauce

1½ cups beer *or* non-alcoholic malt beverage, divided

1 cup *Cattlemen's*® Authentic Smoke House Barbecue Sauce *or* *Cattlemen's*® Award Winning Classic Barbecue Sauce

¼ cup (½ stick) butter

COMBINE barbecue seasoning and chili powder. Rub mixture thoroughly into beef. Place meat, fat-side up, into disposable foil pan. Cover and refrigerate 1 to 3 hours. Just before using, prepare mop sauce by combining **FRANK'S® RedHot®** Original Cayenne Pepper Sauce and *1 cup* beer; set aside.

PREPARE grill for indirect cooking over medium-low heat (250°F). If desired, toss soaked wood chips over coals or heat source. Place pan with meat in center of grill over indirect heat. Cover grill. Cook meat over low heat 6 to 7 hours until meat is very tender (190°F internal temperature). Baste with mop sauce once an hour.

COMBINE barbecue sauce, butter and remaining *½ cup* beer. Simmer 5 minutes until slightly thickened. Slice meat and serve with sauce.

Tip: To easily slice meat, cut against the grain using an electric knife.

Rib-Eye Steaks with Sautéed Grape Tomatoes and Brie

MAKES 2 TO 4 SERVINGS

2 beef rib-eye steaks, cut 1-inch thick (about 12 ounces each)

2 cups grape tomato halves (about 10 ounces)

3 tablespoons water

3 teaspoons minced prepared roasted garlic, divided

4 ounces Brie cheese, shredded

2 tablespoons thinly sliced fresh basil

Fresh basil (optional)

1. Combine tomatoes, water and 1 teaspoon garlic in large nonstick skillet. Cook, covered, over medium heat 4 to 5 minutes or until tomatoes are tender, stirring often. Season with salt and pepper, as desired. Remove from skillet; keep warm. Carefully wipe out skillet with paper towels.

2. Press remaining 2 teaspoons garlic evenly onto beef steaks. Place steaks in skillet over medium heat; cook 12 to 15 minutes for medium rare (145°F) to medium (160°F) doneness, turning occasionally.

3. Season with salt and pepper, as desired. Add cheese and basil to tomatoes; stir until well combined. Serve immediately with beef. Garnish with additional basil, if desired.

Courtesy The Beef Checkoff

Cook's Tip: Two beef top loin (strip) steaks, cut 1-inch thick, may be substituted for ribeye steaks. Cook 12 to 15 minutes, turning occasionally.

Cook's Tip: To make Brie cheese easier to shred, place in freezer for about 30 minutes.

Sassy Chicken & Peppers

MAKES 2 SERVINGS

2 teaspoons Mexican seasoning*

2 boneless skinless chicken breasts (about ¼ pound each)

2 teaspoons vegetable oil

1 small red onion, sliced

½ medium red bell pepper, cut into thin strips

½ medium yellow or green bell pepper, cut into thin strips

¼ cup chunky salsa or chipotle salsa

1 tablespoon lime juice

Lime wedges (optional)

*If Mexican seasoning is not available, substitute 1 teaspoon chili powder, ½ teaspoon ground cumin, ½ teaspoon salt and ⅛ teaspoon ground red pepper.

1. Sprinkle Mexican seasoning over both sides of chicken; set aside.

2. Heat oil in large skillet over medium heat. Add onion; cook 3 minutes, stirring occasionally.

3. Add bell peppers; cook 3 minutes, stirring occasionally. Stir salsa and lime juice into vegetables.

4. Push vegetables to edge of skillet. Add chicken to skillet. Cook 5 minutes; turn. Continue to cook 4 minutes or until chicken is no longer pink in center and vegetables are tender.

5. Remove chicken to serving plates; top with vegetable mixture. Garnish with lime wedges.

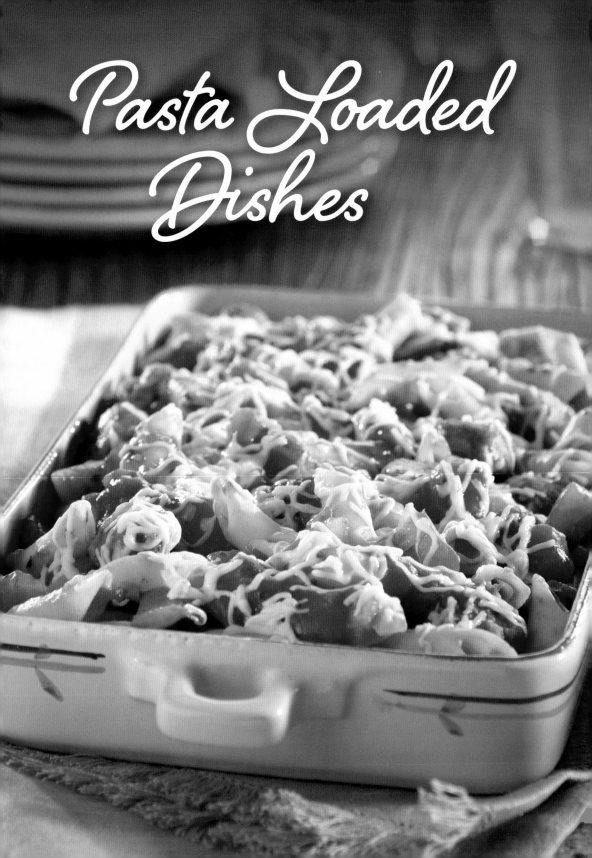

Pasta Loaded Dishes

6 Cheese Italian Sausage & Pasta

MAKES 6 SERVINGS

1 pound mild or hot Italian sausage

1 large onion, coarsely chopped

2 cloves garlic, minced

1 each: large red and green bell peppers, cut into 1-inch squares

1 can (14½ ounces) diced tomatoes or Italian-style tomatoes, undrained

1 can (6 ounces) tomato paste

8 ounces ziti or mostaccioli pasta, cooked and drained

¼ cup chopped fresh basil or 2 teaspoons dried basil

2 cups (8 ounces) SARGENTO® Chef Blends® Shredded 6 Cheese Italian, divided

1. Cut sausage into ½-inch pieces; discard casings. Cook sausage in large skillet over medium heat 5 minutes or until browned on all sides. Pour off drippings. Add onion, garlic and bell peppers; cook 5 minutes or until sausage is cooked through and vegetables are crisp-tender.

2. Add tomatoes and tomato paste; mix well. Stir in pasta, basil and 1 cup cheese. Transfer to 13×9-inch baking dish. Cover and bake in preheated 375°F oven 20 minutes. Uncover; sprinkle remaining cheese evenly over casserole. Continue to bake 5 minutes or until cheese is melted.

Chicken Scaloppine in Alfredo Sauce

MAKES 6 SERVINGS

---

2 tablespoons all-purpose flour

¼ teaspoon salt

¼ teaspoon black pepper

6 boneless, skinless chicken tenderloins (about 1 pound), cut lengthwise in half

1 tablespoon butter

1 tablespoon olive oil

1 cup Alfredo pasta sauce

1 package (12 ounces) uncooked spinach noodles

Slow Cooker Directions

1. Place flour, salt and pepper in large bowl; stir to combine. Add chicken; toss to coat. Heat butter and oil in large skillet over medium-high heat. Add chicken; cook 3 minutes per side or until browned. Remove chicken in single layer to slow cooker.

2. Add Alfredo pasta sauce to slow cooker. Cover; cook on LOW 1 to 1½ hours.

3. Meanwhile, cook noodles according to package directions. Drain; place in large shallow bowl. Spoon chicken and sauce over noodles.

Hearty Beef Lasagna

MAKES 8 TO 10 SERVINGS

1 pound ground beef

1 jar (32 ounces) pasta sauce

2 cups (16 ounces) cottage cheese

1 container (8 ounces) sour cream

8 uncooked lasagna noodles

1½ cups (6 ounces) shredded mozzarella cheese

½ cup grated Parmesan cheese

1 cup water

Fresh basil or thyme (optional)

1. Preheat oven to 350°F.

2. Brown beef in large skillet over medium-high heat 6 to 8 minutes, stirring to break up meat. Drain fat. Reduce heat to low. Add pasta sauce; cook and stir occasionally until heated through. Combine cottage cheese and sour cream in medium bowl; blend well.

3. Spread 1½ cups meat sauce in bottom of 13×9-inch baking pan. Place 4 uncooked noodles over sauce. Top with half of cottage cheese mixture, ¾ cup mozzarella cheese, half of remaining meat sauce and ¼ cup Parmesan cheese. Repeat layers starting with uncooked noodles and topping with remaining ¾ cup mozzarella cheese. Pour water around sides of pan. Cover tightly with foil.

4. Bake 1 hour. Remove foil. Bake, uncovered, 20 minutes or until hot and bubbly. Let stand 15 to 20 minutes before cutting. Garnish with basil.

Hungarian Beef Goulash

MAKES 8 SERVINGS

¼ cup all-purpose flour

1 tablespoon Hungarian sweet paprika

1½ teaspoons salt

½ teaspoon Hungarian hot paprika

½ teaspoon black pepper

2 pounds cubed beef stew meat

¼ cup vegetable oil, divided

1 large onion, chopped

4 cloves garlic, minced

2 cans (about 14 ounces each) beef broth

1 can (about 14 ounces) stewed tomatoes, undrained

1 cup water

1 tablespoon dried marjoram

1 large green bell pepper, chopped

3 cups uncooked thin egg noodles

Sour cream

1. Combine flour, sweet paprika, salt, hot paprika and black pepper in large resealable food storage bag. Add half of beef. Seal bag; shake to coat well. Remove beef; set aside. Repeat with remaining beef.

2. Heat 4½ teaspoons oil in Dutch oven over medium heat. Add half of beef; cook 6 to 8 minutes or until browned on all sides. Remove to large bowl. Repeat with 4½ teaspoons oil and remaining beef; remove to same bowl.

3. Heat remaining 1 tablespoon oil in same Dutch oven. Add onion and garlic; cook 8 minutes or until tender, stirring often.

4. Return beef and any accumulated juices to Dutch oven. Add broth, tomatoes with juice, water and marjoram. Bring to a boil over medium-high heat. Reduce heat; cover and simmer 1½ hours or until meat is tender, stirring once.

5. Stir in bell pepper and noodles; cover. Simmer 8 minutes or until noodles are tender, stirring once. Ladle into soup bowls; top with sour cream.

Baked Italian Chicken & Pasta

MAKES 4 SERVINGS

1 can (10¾ ounces) CAMPBELL'S® Condensed Tomato Soup

1⅓ cups water

1 teaspoon dried basil leaves, crushed

2 cups **uncooked** corkscrew-shaped pasta (rotini)

4 skinless, boneless chicken breast halves (about 1 pound)

½ cup shredded mozzarella cheese

1. Stir the soup, water, basil and pasta in a 2-quart shallow baking dish. Top with the chicken. Sprinkle with the cheese and additional basil, if desired. Cover the baking dish.

2. Bake at 350°F. for 45 minutes or until the chicken is cooked through and the pasta is tender.

Tuna-Macaroni Casserole

MAKES 6 SERVINGS

1 cup mayonnaise

1 cup (4 ounces) shredded Swiss cheese

½ cup milk

¼ cup chopped onion

¼ cup chopped red bell pepper

⅛ teaspoon black pepper

2 cans (about 6 ounces each) tuna, drained and flaked

1 package (about 10 ounces) frozen peas

2 cups shell pasta or elbow macaroni, cooked and drained

½ cup plain dry bread crumbs

2 tablespoons melted butter

Chopped fresh parsley (optional)

1. Preheat oven to 350°F.

2. Combine mayonnaise, cheese, milk, onion, bell pepper and black pepper in large bowl. Add tuna, peas and pasta, toss to coat well. Spoon into 2-quart casserole.

3. Mix bread crumbs with butter in small bowl and sprinkle over top of casserole. Bake 30 to 40 minutes or until heated through. Garnish with chopped parsley.

Spaghetti & Meatballs

MAKES 4 SERVINGS

Nonstick cooking spray

6 ounces uncooked multigrain or whole wheat spaghetti

¾ pound ground beef

¼ pound hot turkey Italian sausage, casings removed

1 egg white

2 tablespoons plain dry bread crumbs

1 teaspoon dried oregano

2 cups tomato-basil pasta sauce

3 tablespoons thinly sliced fresh basil

2 tablespoons grated Parmesan cheese

1. Preheat oven to 450°F. Spray medium baking sheet with cooking spray. Cook spaghetti according to package directions, omitting salt and fat. Drain and keep warm.

2. Combine beef, sausage, egg white, bread crumbs and oregano in medium bowl. Shape mixture into 16 (1½-inch) meatballs. Place on prepared baking sheet; coat with cooking spray. Bake 12 minutes, turning once.

3. Pour pasta sauce into large skillet. Add meatballs; cook over medium heat 9 minutes or until sauce is heated through and meatballs are cooked through (160°F), stirring occasionally. Divide spaghetti among four plates. Top with meatballs and sauce; sprinkle with basil and cheese.

Braised Turkey Breasts with Lemon-Artichoke Heart Sauce

MAKES 6 SERVINGS

2 bone-in, skin-on turkey breast halves (about 2 pounds each)

2 teaspoons salt, plus additional for seasoning

¼ teaspoon black pepper, plus additional for seasoning

½ cup all-purpose flour

4 teaspoons vegetable oil, divided

4 large shallots, peeled and thinly sliced

½ cup dry sherry

1 lemon, sliced into ¼-inch-thick slices

2 tablespoons capers, rinsed and drained

4 sprigs fresh thyme

1½ cups chicken broth

2 cans (about 14 ounces each) artichoke hearts, drained

2 tablespoons finely chopped parsley

Hot cooked egg noodles (optional)

Slow Cooker Directions

1. Season both sides of turkey breasts with salt and pepper. Dredge in flour, shaking off excess. Warm 2 teaspoons oil in large skillet over medium-high heat. Add 1 turkey breast half; cook 4 minutes or until browned on both sides. Remove to slow cooker. Repeat with remaining 2 teaspoons oil and second turkey breast; remove to slow cooker.

2. Reduce heat to medium. Add shallots to skillet; cook 4 minutes or until softened and just beginning to brown. Add sherry; stir to scrape up any browned bits from bottom of pan. Cook until pan is almost dry, about 30 seconds, then pour over turkey breasts. Add lemon slices, capers, thyme, 2 teaspoons salt and ¼ teaspoon pepper. Pour in broth. Cover; cook on LOW 6 hours or until turkey breasts are tender and nearly falling off the bone.

3. Remove turkey breasts; set aside to cool 10 minutes. Remove and discard skin and bones.

4. Remove and discard thyme. Skim fat from sauce. Stir in artichoke hearts and parsley. Season to taste with salt and pepper. Slice turkey. Serve on hot cooked egg noodles topped with sauce.

Cheesy Italian Noodle Bake

MAKES 8 TO 10 SERVINGS

4 packages (3 ounces each) ramen noodles, any flavor*

1 pound sweet Italian sausage, casings removed

2 teaspoons olive oil

1 cup diced onion

1 cup diced red bell pepper

1 teaspoon minced garlic

1 can (about 15 ounces) tomato sauce

½ cup thinly sliced fresh basil

2 cups (8 ounces) shredded mozzarella cheese

Discard seasoning packets.

1. Preheat oven to 400°F. Grease 13×9-inch baking dish.

2. Cook noodles according to package directions. Drain and rinse under cold running water. Remove to large bowl.

3. Brown sausage in large skillet over medium-high heat 8 minutes or until well browned, stirring to break up meat. Drain on paper towel-lined plate. Remove to bowl with noodles.

4. Heat oil in skillet. Add onion and bell pepper; cook and stir 6 minutes or until softened. Add garlic; cook 30 seconds. Remove to bowl. Add tomato sauce and basil; stir until well combined.

5. Spread mixture evenly in prepared dish. Sprinkle with cheese. Bake 25 to 30 minutes or until bubbly and cheese is golden brown. Let stand 5 minutes before serving.

Classic Beef & Noodles

MAKES 8 SERVINGS

1 tablespoon
  vegetable oil

2 pounds cubed beef
  stew meat

¼ pound mushrooms,
  sliced into halves

2 tablespoons
  chopped onion

2 cloves garlic, minced

1 teaspoon salt

1 teaspoon dried
  oregano

½ teaspoon black
  pepper

¼ teaspoon dried
  marjoram

1 whole bay leaf

1½ cups beef broth

⅓ cup dry sherry

1 cup (8 ounces) sour
  cream

½ cup all-purpose flour

¼ cup water

4 cups hot cooked
  wide egg noodles

  Chopped fresh
  parsley (optional)

Slow Cooker Directions

1. Heat oil in large skillet. Add beef; cook 6 to 8 minutes or until browned on all sides. (Work in batches, if necessary.) Drain and discard fat.

2. Combine beef, mushrooms, onion, garlic, salt, oregano, pepper, marjoram and bay leaf in slow cooker. Pour in broth and sherry. Cover; cook on LOW 8 to 10 hours or on HIGH 4 to 5 hours. Remove and discard bay leaf.

3. Combine sour cream, flour and water in small bowl. Stir about 1 cup liquid from slow cooker into sour cream mixture. Add mixture to slow cooker. Cook, uncovered, on HIGH 30 minutes or until thickened and bubbly. Serve over noodles. Garnish with parsley.

Skillet Lasagna with Vegetables

MAKES 6 SERVINGS

½ pound hot Italian turkey sausage, casings removed

½ pound ground turkey

2 stalks celery, sliced

⅓ cup chopped onion

2 cups marinara sauce

1⅓ cups water

4 ounces uncooked bowtie (farfalle) pasta

1 medium zucchini, halved lengthwise and cut into ½-inch-thick slices (2 cups)

¾ cup chopped green or yellow bell pepper

½ cup ricotta cheese

2 tablespoons finely grated Parmesan cheese

½ cup (2 ounces) shredded mozzarella cheese

1. Cook and stir sausage, turkey, celery and onion in large skillet over medium-high heat until turkey is no longer pink. Drain fat. Stir in marinara sauce and water. Bring to a boil. Add pasta; stir. Reduce heat to medium-low; cover and simmer 12 minutes.

2. Stir in zucchini and bell pepper; cover and simmer 2 minutes. Uncover and simmer 4 to 6 minutes or until vegetables are crisp-tender.

3. Meanwhile, combine ricotta and Parmesan cheeses in small bowl. Drop by rounded teaspoonfuls on top of mixture in skillet. Sprinkle with mozzarella. Remove from heat; cover and let stand 10 minutes.

Creamy Chicken

MAKES 3 SERVINGS

- 3 boneless skinless chicken breasts *or* 6 boneless skinless chicken thighs

- 2 cans (10¾ ounces each) condensed cream of chicken soup, undiluted

- 1 can (about 14 ounces) chicken broth

- 1 can (4 ounces) sliced mushrooms, drained

- ½ medium onion, diced

  Salt and black pepper

  Hot cooked wide egg noodles (optional)

Slow Cooker Directions

Place chicken, soup, broth, mushrooms and onion in slow cooker. Cover; cook on LOW 6 to 8 hours. Season to taste with salt and pepper. Serve over noodles, if desired.

Tip: If desired, you may add 8 ounces of cubed pasteurized process cheese product before serving.

Italian Tomato Bake

MAKES 6 SERVINGS

1 pound sweet Italian sausage, cut into ½-inch slices

2 tablespoons butter

1 cup chopped onion

4 cups cooked egg noodles

2 cups frozen broccoli florets, thawed and drained

2 cups prepared pasta sauce

½ cup diced plum tomatoes

2 cloves garlic, minced

3 plum tomatoes, sliced

1 cup (8 ounces) ricotta cheese

⅓ cup grated Parmesan cheese

1 teaspoon dried oregano

1. Preheat oven to 350°F. Cook sausage in large skillet over medium heat about 10 minutes or until barely pink in center. Drain on paper towels; set aside. Drain fat from skillet.

2. Add butter and onion to skillet; cook and stir until onion is tender. Combine onion, noodles, broccoli, pasta sauce, diced tomatoes and garlic in large bowl; mix well. Remove to 13×9-inch baking dish.

3. Top with sausage and tomato slices. Place 1 heaping tablespoonful ricotta cheese on each tomato slice. Sprinkle with Parmesan cheese and oregano. Bake 35 minutes or until hot and bubbly.

Broccoli and Beef Pasta

MAKES 4 SERVINGS

1 pound ground beef

2 cloves garlic, minced

1 can (about 14 ounces) beef broth

1 medium onion, thinly sliced

1 cup uncooked rotini pasta

½ teaspoon dried basil

½ teaspoon dried oregano

½ teaspoon dried thyme

1 can (15 ounces) Italian-style tomatoes, undrained

2 cups broccoli florets *or* 1 package (10 ounces) frozen broccoli, thawed

¾ cup (3 ounces) shredded Cheddar cheese or grated Parmesan cheese

1. Brown beef and garlic in Dutch oven over medium-high heat 6 to 8 minutes, stirring to break up meat. Drain fat. Remove meat to large bowl; set aside.

2. Add broth, onion, pasta, basil, oregano and thyme to Dutch oven. Bring to a boil; boil 10 minutes. Stir in tomatoes with juice and broccoli. Reduce heat to medium-high and simmer, uncovered, 6 to 8 minutes, stirring occasionally, until broccoli is crisp-tender and pasta is tender. Return meat to Dutch oven and simmer 3 to 4 minutes or until heated through.

3. Remove to serving platter with slotted spoon. Sprinkle with cheese. Cover with lid or tent with foil until cheese melts. Meanwhile, bring liquid left in Dutch oven to a boil over high heat. Boil until thick and reduced to 3 to 4 tablespoons. Spoon over pasta mixture.

Serving Suggestion: Serve with garlic bread.

Three Pepper Pasta Sauce

MAKES 4 TO 6 SERVINGS

1 *each* red, yellow and green bell pepper, cut into 1-inch pieces

2 cans (about 14 ounces each) diced tomatoes, undrained

1 cup chopped onion

1 can (6 ounces) tomato paste

4 cloves garlic, minced

2 tablespoons olive oil

1 teaspoon dried basil

1 teaspoon dried oregano

½ teaspoon salt

¼ teaspoon red pepper flakes or black pepper

Hot cooked pasta

Shredded Parmesan or Romano cheese

Slow Cooker Directions

1. Combine bell pepper, tomatoes with juice, onion, tomato paste, garlic, oil, basil, oregano, salt and red pepper flakes in slow cooker. Cover; cook on LOW 7 to 8 hours or until vegetables are tender.

2. Adjust seasonings, if desired. Serve with pasta and cheese.

From the Bar

< *Whiskey Smash*

MAKES 1 SERVING

2 lemon quarters

8 fresh mint leaves, plus additional for garnish

½ ounce Simple Syrup (recipe follows)

2 ounces bourbon

Muddle lemon quarters, 8 mint leaves and Simple Syrup in cocktail shaker. Add bourbon; shake until blended. Strain into old fashioned glass filled with crushed ice; garnish with additional mint.

Simple Syrup: Bring 1 cup water to a boil; stir in 1 cup sugar. Reduce heat to low; stir constantly until sugar is dissolved. Cool to room temperature; store syrup in glass jar in refrigerator.

Rusty Nail

MAKES 1 SERVING

1½ ounces Scotch

1 ounce Drambuie

Stir together Scotch and Drambuie in ice-filled old fashioned glass.

Cosmopolitan >

MAKES 1 SERVING

2 ounces vodka or lemon-flavored vodka

1 ounce triple sec

1 ounce cranberry juice

½ ounce lime juice

Lime wedge

Fill cocktail shaker half full with ice; add vodka, triple sec and juices. Shake until blended; strain into chilled cocktail glass. Garnish with lime wedge.

Sherry Cobbler

MAKES 1 SERVING

½ teaspoon orange liqueur

½ teaspoon Simple Syrup (page 155)

4 ounces dry sherry (amontillado or oloroso)

Orange slice

Fill large wine glass or old fashioned glass three fourths full with crushed ice; add liqueur and simple syrup. Stir until blended. Gently stir in sherry; garnish with orange slice.

Lime Rickey

MAKES 1 SERVING

Lime wedges

2 ounces vodka

2 ounces gin

2 ounces lime juice

Club soda

Sprig fresh mint
(optional)

Fill highball glass with lime wedges; add vodka, gin and lime juice. Top with club soda to fill. Garnish with mint.

Raspberry Rickey: Place ⅓ cup fresh raspberries in small bowl; sprinkle with 2 teaspoons sugar. Add lime juice; let sit 10 minutes. Press through sieve to remove seeds. Combine raspberry mixture, 2 ounces raspberry-flavored vodka and 2 ounces gin in ice-filled old fashioned glass. Fill with club soda. Garnish with fresh raspberries and mint leaves.

Brandy Collins >

MAKES 1 SERVING

2 ounces brandy

1 ounce lemon juice

1 teaspoon powdered sugar

3 ounces chilled club soda

Orange slice and maraschino cherry

Fill cocktail shaker half full with ice; add brandy, lemon juice and powdered sugar. Shake until blended; strain into ice-filled Collins glass. Add club soda; stir until blended. Garnish with orange slice and maraschino cherry.

Watermelon Refresher

MAKES 4 SERVINGS

6 cups ripe seedless watermelon chunks

¼ cup lemon juice

1 cup chilled champagne

1. Place watermelon in blender; process in two batches until smooth. Strain through sieve into large bowl. Refrigerate until cold.

2. Combine 3 cups watermelon juice and lemon juice in pitcher. Gently stir in champagne. Serve over ice, if desired.

Gin Sour >

MAKES 1 SERVING

- 2 ounces gin
- ¾ ounce lemon juice
- ¾ ounce Simple Syrup (page 155)
- Lemon twist

Fill cocktail shaker with ice; add gin, lemon juice and simple syrup. Shake until blended; strain into chilled martini glass. Garnish with lemon twist.

Fitzgerald: Add 2 dashes Angostura bitters to cocktail shaker; proceed as directed.

West Side

MAKES 1 SERVING

- 2 ounces lemon-flavored vodka
- 1 ounce lemon juice
- ½ ounce Simple Syrup (page 155)
- 1 sprig fresh mint
- Chilled club soda

Fill cocktail shaker with ice; add vodka, lemon juice, simple syrup and mint. Shake until blended. Top with splash of club soda; strain into chilled cocktail glass.

Bloody Mary >

MAKES 1 SERVING

Dash *each*
Worcestershire
sauce, hot pepper
sauce, celery salt,
black pepper and
salt

3 ounces tomato juice

1½ ounces vodka

½ ounce lemon juice

Celery stalk with
leaves, pickle spear,
lemon slice and/or
green olives

Fill highball glass with ice; add dashes of Worcestershire sauce, hot pepper sauce, celery salt, black pepper and salt. Add tomato juice, vodka and lemon juice; stir gently until blended. Serve with desired garnishes.

Eldorado

MAKES 1 SERVING

---

2 ounces tequila

1 tablespoon honey

1½ ounces lemon juice

Lemon or orange
slice

Fill cocktail shaker half full with ice; add tequila, honey and lemon juice. Shake until blended; strain into ice-filled old fashioned or Collins glass. Garnish with lemon slice.

Sazerac >

MAKES 1 SERVING

---

2 ounces whiskey

¼ ounce anise-flavored liqueur

½ ounce Simple Syrup (page 155)

Dash of bitters

Fill cocktail shaker half full with ice; add whiskey, liqueur, Simple Syrup and bitters. Stir until blended; strain into old fashioned glass.

Buck

MAKES 1 SERVING

Juice of ¼ lime

1½ ounces gin

Ginger ale

Fill old fashioned glass with ice; squeeze lime juice over ice and drop lime into glass. Add gin and ginger ale to fill; stir gently.

Bellini >

MAKES 1 SERVING

3 ounces peach nectar*

4 ounces chilled
champagne or dry
sparkling wine

*Or peel and pit a ripe
medium peach and purée in
blender.*

Pour peach nectar into chilled champagne flute; slowly pour in champagne and stir gently.

Pomegranate Mimosa

MAKES 8 SERVINGS

2 cups chilled
pomegranate juice

1 bottle (750 ml)
chilled champagne

Pomegranate seeds
(optional)

Pour pomegranate juice into eight champagne flutes; top with champagne. Garnish with pomegranate seeds.

Manhattan >

MAKES 1 SERVING

---

2 ounces whiskey

1 ounce sweet
vermouth

Dash Angostura
bitters

Maraschino cherry

Fill cocktail shaker half full with ice; add whiskey, vermouth and bitters. Stir until blended; strain into chilled cocktail glass. Garnish with maraschino cherry.

Cherry Collins

MAKES 1 SERVING

---

2 ounces cherry-
flavored vodka

¾ ounce lemon juice

¾ ounce Simple Syrup
(page 155)

Club soda

Fresh cherries

Fill highball glass with ice; add vodka, lemon juice and simple syrup. Stir until blended; top with club soda. Garnish with cherries.

Whiskey Sour >

MAKES 1 SERVING

---

2 ounces whiskey

Juice of ½ lemon

1 teaspoon powdered sugar

Lemon or orange slice and maraschino cherry

Fill cocktail shaker half full with ice; add whiskey, lemon juice and powdered sugar. Shake until blended; strain into ice-filled old fashioned glass. Garnish with lemon slice and maraschino cherry.

Variation: Fill cocktail shaker half full with ice; add 4 ounces sweet and sour mix and 1½ ounces whiskey. Shake until blended; strain into ice-filled old fashioned glass. Garnish with lemon slice and maraschino cherry.

Sweet Ruby

MAKES 1 SERVING

---

1 ounce ruby port

¾ ounce amaretto

2 dashes Angostura bitters

Fill mixing glass or cocktail shaker with ice; add port, amaretto and bitters. Stir 10 seconds; strain into chilled old fashioned glass half full of ice.

Mojito >

MAKES 2 SERVINGS

---

8 fresh mint leaves

12 ounces lime juice

2 teaspoons superfine sugar or powdered sugar

3 ounces light rum

Soda water

2 lime slices

Sprigs fresh mint (optional)

Combine half of mint leaves, lime juice and sugar in each of two highball glasses; mash with wooden spoon or muddler. Fill glasses with ice. Pour rum over ice; top with soda water. Garnish with lime slices and mint sprigs.

Gin St. Clement's

MAKES 1 SERVING

1½ ounces gin

1 ounce lemon juice

1 ounce orange juice

2 ounces tonic water

Orange and/or lemon slices

Fill Collins or highball glass with ice; add gin, lemon juice and orange juice. Top with tonic water; stir until blended. Garnish with orange slice.

Martini >

MAKES 1 SERVING

- 2 ounces gin or vodka
- ½ ounce dry vermouth

Fill cocktail shaker half full with ice; add gin and vermouth. Stir or shake until blended; strain into chilled cocktail glass.

Dirty Martini: Add 1 to 2 teaspoons olive brine to Martini; garnish with olive.

Gibson: Garnish Martini with cocktail onion.

Viceroy

MAKES 1 SERVING

- 1½ ounces pisco
- 1 ounce Lillet Blanc
- ½ ounce lime juice
- ½ ounce Simple Syrup (page 155)
- 1½ ounces tonic water
- Sprig fresh mint

Combine pisco, Lillet Blanc, lime juice and simple syrup in highball glass filled with ice. Top with tonic water; stir gently until blended. Garnish with mint.

Long Island Iced Tea

MAKES 1 SERVING

½ ounce vodka

½ ounce tequila

½ ounce light rum

½ ounce gin

½ ounce triple sec

1 ounce lemon juice

1 teaspoon sugar

Chilled cola

Lemon wedge and
maraschino cherry

Fill cocktail shaker half full with ice; add vodka, tequila, rum, gin, triple sec, lemon juice and sugar. Shake until blended; strain into ice-filled highball glass. Fill with cola; garnish with lemon wedge and maraschino cherry.

Sidecar >

MAKES 1 SERVING

---

2 ounces brandy or Cognac

2 ounces orange-flavored liqueur

½ ounce lemon juice

Fill cocktail shaker half full with ice; add brandy, liqueur and lemon juice. Shake until blended; strain into chilled cocktail glass.

Snake Bite

MAKES 1 SERVING

---

8 ounces ale

8 ounces hard cider

Pour ale into chilled pint glass; top with cider. *Do not stir.*

Tom Collins >

MAKES 1 SERVING

- 2 ounces gin
- 1 ounce lemon juice
- 1 teaspoon superfine sugar
- 3 ounces chilled club soda

  Lemon slice

Fill cocktail shaker half full with ice; add gin, lemon juice and sugar. Shake until blended; strain into ice-filled Collins glass. Fill with club soda. Garnish with lemon slice.

Hunter's Cocktail

MAKES 1 SERVING

- 1½ ounces rye whiskey
- ½ ounce cherry-flavored brandy

  Maraschino cherry

Fill old fashioned glass half full with ice; add whiskey and brandy. Stir until blended; garnish with maraschino cherry.

Index

Acknowledgments

The publisher would like to thank the companies and organizations listed below for the use of their recipes and photographs in this publication.

The Beef Checkoff

Campbell Soup Company

Reckitt Benckiser LLC

Riviana Foods Inc.

Sargento® Foods, Inc.

Unilever

METRIC CONVERSION CHART

VOLUME MEASUREMENTS (dry)

$^1/_8$ teaspoon = 0.5 mL
$^1/_4$ teaspoon = 1 mL
$^1/_2$ teaspoon = 2 mL
$^3/_4$ teaspoon = 4 mL
1 teaspoon = 5 mL
1 tablespoon = 15 mL
2 tablespoons = 30 mL
$^1/_4$ cup = 60 mL
$^1/_3$ cup = 75 mL
$^1/_2$ cup = 125 mL
$^2/_3$ cup = 150 mL
$^3/_4$ cup = 175 mL
1 cup = 250 mL
2 cups = 1 pint = 500 mL
3 cups = 750 mL
4 cups = 1 quart = 1 L

VOLUME MEASUREMENTS (fluid)

1 fluid ounce (2 tablespoons) = 30 mL
4 fluid ounces ($^1/_2$ cup) = 125 mL
8 fluid ounces (1 cup) = 250 mL
12 fluid ounces (1$^1/_2$ cups) = 375 mL
16 fluid ounces (2 cups) = 500 mL

WEIGHTS (mass)

$^1/_2$ ounce = 15 g
1 ounce = 30 g
3 ounces = 90 g
4 ounces = 120 g
8 ounces = 225 g
10 ounces = 285 g
12 ounces = 360 g
16 ounces = 1 pound = 450 g

DIMENSIONS

$^1/_{16}$ inch = 2 mm
$^1/_8$ inch = 3 mm
$^1/_4$ inch = 6 mm
$^1/_2$ inch = 1.5 cm
$^3/_4$ inch = 2 cm
1 inch = 2.5 cm

OVEN TEMPERATURES

250°F = 120°C
275°F = 140°C
300°F = 150°C
325°F = 160°C
350°F = 180°C
375°F = 190°C
400°F = 200°C
425°F = 220°C
450°F = 230°C

BAKING PAN SIZES

Utensil	Size in Inches/Quarts	Metric Volume	Size in Centimeters
Baking or Cake Pan (square or rectangular)	8×8×2	2 L	20×20×5
	9×9×2	2.5 L	23×23×5
	12×8×2	3 L	30×20×5
	13×9×2	3.5 L	33×23×5
Loaf Pan	8×4×3	1.5 L	20×10×7
	9×5×3	2 L	23×13×7
Round Layer Cake Pan	8×1½	1.2 L	20×4
	9×1½	1.5 L	23×4
Pie Plate	8×1¼	750 mL	20×3
	9×1¼	1 L	23×3
Baking Dish or Casserole	1 quart	1 L	—
	1½ quart	1.5 L	—
	2 quart	2 L	—